INTRODUCTION

The ability to sight-read fluently is a most important part of your training as a pianist, whether you intend to play professionally, or simply for enjoyment. Yet the *study* of sight-reading is often badly neglected by young players and is frequently regarded as no more than a rather unpleasant side-line. If you become a good sight-reader you will be able to learn pieces more quickly, accompany your friends, play piano duets and chamber music, all with confidence and assurance. Also, in grade examinations, good performance in the sight-reading test will result in useful extra marks!

Using the workbook

The purpose of this workbook is to incorporate sight-reading regularly into your practice and lessons, and to help you prepare for the sight-reading test in grade examinations. It offers you a progressive series of enjoyable and stimulating stages in which, with careful work, you should show considerable improvement from week to week.

Each stage consists of two parts: firstly, exercises which you should prepare in advance, along with a short piece with questions; and secondly, an unprepared test, to be found at the end of the book.

Your teacher will mark your work according to accuracy. Each stage carries a maximum of 50 marks and your work will be assessed as follows:

> 2 marks for each of the six questions relating to the prepared piece (total 12)
> 18 marks for the prepared piece itself.
> 20 marks for the unprepared test. (Teachers should devise a similar series of questions for the unprepared test, and take the answers into account when allocating a final mark.)

Space is given at the end of each stage for you to keep a running total of your marks as you progress. If you are scoring 40 or more each time you are doing well!

At the top of the first page in each stage you will see one or two new features to be introduced. There are then normally four different types of exercise:

1 **Rhythmic exercises** It is very important that you should be able to feel and maintain a steady beat. These exercises will help develop this ability. There are at least four ways of doing these exercises: clap or tap the lower line (the beat) while singing the upper line to 'la'; tap the lower line with your foot and clap the upper line; on a table or flat surface, tap the lower line with one hand and the upper line with the other; 'play' the lower line on a metronome and clap or tap the upper line.

2 **Melodic exercises** Fluent sight-reading depends on recognising melodic shapes at first glance. These shapes are often related to scales and arpeggios. Before you begin, always notice the *key-signature* and the notes affected by it, along with any accidentals.

3 **A prepared piece with questions** You should prepare carefully both the piece and the questions, which are to help you think about and understand the piece before you play it. Put your answers in the spaces provided.

4 **An unprepared piece** Finally, your teacher will give you an *unprepared* test to be read at *sight*. Make sure you have read the *Sight-Reading Checklist* on page 26 before you begin each piece.

Remember to count throughout each piece and to keep going at a steady and even tempo. Always try to look ahead, at least to the next note or beat.

STAGE 1

RHYTHMIC EXERCISES

1

2

3

MELODIC EXERCISES

1

2

3

This music is copyright. Photocopying is illegal

PREPARED PIECE

1 How many beats are there in each bar?

2 What is the key of this piece?

3 How many beats is each crotchet (♩) worth?

4 How many beats is each crotchet rest (𝄽) worth?

5 What does *Andante* mean?

6 What does *f* (*forte*) indicate?

Total:

Andante

Unprepared tests page 26

Mark:

Prepared work total:

Unprepared:

Total:

*The mark boxes are to be filled in by your teacher.

STAGE 2

Small leaps

RHYTHMIC EXERCISES

1

2

3

MELODIC EXERCISES

1

2

3

PREPARED PIECE

1 How many beats are there in each bar?

2 What is the key of this piece?

3 How many beats is each crotchet (♩) worth?

4 How many beats is each crotchet rest (𝄽) worth?

5 What does *Moderato* mean?

6 What does *f (forte)* indicate?

Total:

Moderato

Unprepared tests page 27

Mark:

Prepared work total:

Unprepared:

Total:

Running totals:

1   2

STAGE 3

$\frac{3}{4}$ 𝅗𝅥.

G major

RHYTHMIC EXERCISES

MELODIC EXERCISES

PREPARED PIECE

1 What does $\frac{3}{4}$ indicate?

2 How many beats is each minim (𝅗𝅥) worth?

3 How many beats is each dotted minim (𝅗𝅥·) worth?

4 In which key is the piece written?

5 What does *mf* (*mezzo-forte*) indicate?

6 What is the meaning of *Andante*?

Total:

Andante

Unprepared tests page 28

Mark:

Prepared work total:

Unprepared:

Total:

Running totals:

1	2	3

STAGE 4

F major

RHYTHMIC EXERCISES

1

2

3

4

MELODIC EXERCISES

1

2

3

12

PREPARED PIECE

1 In which key is this piece written?

2 Mark a cross above the B flats.

3 What do you notice about the way the dynamic levels are split between the hands?

4 What does *Andante* mean?

5 What will you count?

6 What is the interval formed by the first two notes (left hand)?

Total:

Andante

Unprepared tests page 29

Mark:

Prepared work total:

Unprepared:

Total:

Running totals:

1	2	3	4

STAGE 5

Tied notes

RHYTHMIC EXERCISES

MELODIC EXERCISES

PREPARED PIECE

1 How many beats is each dotted minim (𝅗𝅥·) worth?

2 Mark any notes affected by the key signature?

3 Mark a tied note with an asterisk.

4 What does *p* (*piano*) indicate?

5 What does indicate?

6 What is the meaning of *Moderato*?

Total:

Moderato

Unprepared tests page 30

Mark:

Prepared work total:

Unprepared:

Total:

Running totals:

1	2	3	4	5

STAGE 6

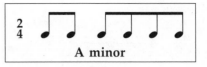

RHYTHMIC EXERCISES

MELODIC EXERCISES

PREPARED PIECE

1 What does $\frac{4}{4}$ indicate? *The beat – $\frac{4}{4}$ = 4 crotchets in A Bar*

2 Clap the following rhythm:

3 In which bars does the above rhythm occur?

4 Mark the accidentals with a cross.

5 What does the sign ——— (*crescendo*) indicate?

6 What is the meaning of *Allegro moderato*? *moderately quick*

Total:

Allegro moderato

Unprepared tests page 31   Mark:

Prepared work total:

Unprepared:

Total:

Running totals:

1	2	3	4	5	6

STAGE 7

RHYTHMIC EXERCISES

MELODIC EXERCISES

22

PREPARED PIECE

1 In which key is this piece written?

2 How many beats will you count in each bar?

3 What is the letter-name of the last note (right hand)?

4 Is this a happy or a sad piece?

5 How will you achieve the necessary character?

6 In how many bars does the rhythm of bar 2 re-occur?

Total:

Allegretto

Unprepared tests page 32

Mark:

Prepared work total:

Unprepared:

Total:

Running totals:

1	2	3	4	5	6	7

STAGE 8

RHYTHMIC EXERCISES

1

2

3

MELODIC EXERCISES

1

2

3

PREPARED PIECE

1 In which key is this piece written?

2 Mark the C sharps with a cross.

3 What do the dots under and over the notes indicate?

4 What does *Allegretto* mean?

5 What does *cresc.* (*crescendo*) indicate?

6 Mark a tied note with an asterisk.

Total:

Unprepared tests page 33

Mark:

Prepared work total:

Unprepared:

Total:

Running totals:

1	2	3	4	5	6	7	8

CONCLUSION

A sight-reading checklist

Before you begin to play a piece at sight, always remember to consider the following:

1   Look at the time-signature, and decide how you will count the piece.

2   Look at the key-signature, and find the notes which need raising or lowering.

3   Notice any accidentals that may occur.

4   Notice scale or arpeggio patterns.

5   Work out leger-line notes if necessary.

6   Notice dynamic levels and other markings.

7   Look at the tempo mark and decide what speed to play.

8   Count one bar before you begin, to establish the speed.

When performing your sight-reading piece, always remember to:

1   CONTINUE TO COUNT THROUGHOUT THE PIECE.

2   Keep going at a steady and even tempo.

3   Ignore mistakes.

4   Look ahead – at least to the next note.

5   Keep your hands in position on the keyboard during rests.

6   Play *musically*.

UNPREPARED TESTS
STAGE 1

1   Moderato

2   Allegretto

3 Allegretto

4 Andante

STAGE 2

1 Allegretto

2 Moderato

3 Allegretto

4 Moderato

STAGE 3

1 Andante

2 Allegretto

3 Con moto

4 Andante

STAGE 4

1 Moderato

2 Allegretto

3 Marziale

4 Cantabile

STAGE 5

1 Moderato

2 Andante

3 Boldly

4 Allegretto

STAGE 6

1 Andante

2 Allegretto

3 Allegro

4 Con moto

STAGE 7

1 Allegro

2 Moderato

3 Alla marcia

4 Ritmico